HOW TO TURN WAR INTO PEACE

A Child's Guide To Conflict Resolution

Also by Louise Armstrong

HOW TO TURN LEMONS INTO MONEY
A Child's Guide to Economics

HOW TO TURN UP INTO DOWN INTO UP
A Child's Guide to Inflation, Depression, and Economic Recovery

ARTHUR GETS WHAT HE SPILLS

HARCOURT BRACE JOVANOVICH
NEW YORK AND LONDON

A Let Me Read book

HOW TO TURN WAR INTO Peace

by Louise Armstrong
illustrated by Bill Basso

Requests for permission to make copies of
any part of the work should be mailed to:
Permissions, Harcourt Brace Jovanovich, Inc.,
757 Third Avenue, New York, New York 10017

Printed in the United States of America

LIBRARY OF CONGRESS CATALOGING IN PUBLICATION DATA

Armstrong, Louise.
How to turn war into peace.
(A Let me read book)
1. Social conflict–Juvenile literature.
2. Violence–Juvenile literature.
3. War–Juvenile literature.
4. Peace–Juvenile literature.
I. Basso, Bill. II. Title.
HM291.A77 301.6′3 79-11797
ISBN 0-15-236840-X
ISBN 0-15-642206-9 pbk.

First edition
B C D E

This is Susie. If she's building her sand castle right next to yours, you're in a POTENTIAL TROUBLE SPOT.

That means Susie's digging might clog your moat, creating a INCIDENT.

If you yell "Move!"—you have a DISPUTE.

If she yells, *"You* move!"—you have a CONFLICT.

Susie is your ADVERSARY.

If she waves her shovel at you, this is a WARNING SIGNAL.

If she says she's going to throw it, this is a THREAT.

What she's threatening is VIOLENCE.

If you say she couldn't even hit you, this is EVALUATING THE OPPOSITION'S FORCE.

But if you say with your aim you *could* hit *her,* you are using a WEAPON DETERRENT.

Your aim is the DETERRENT.
Your shovel is the
WEAPON.

Now if you throw your shovel and miss, you have lost CREDIBILITY.

If she throws hers and hits you, this is a SUCCESSFUL REPRISAL.

If it makes you mad, you might threaten INVASION.

Or you might call over some friends and ADDRESS YOUR ALLIES.

If, while you're talking, Susie pours water on your turret, this is a SURPRISE ATTACK.

You will MOBILIZE YOUR TROOPS.

Decide on your GOAL.
(To defeat Susie.)

Plan your STRATEGY.
(To drive her off the beach.)

Outline your TACTICS.
(To throw stuff at her castle.)

Now if everyone's hungry and you break for lunch, this is a TEMPORARY CEASE FIRE.
If Susie kicks sand in your sandwich, this is FRESH PROVOCATION,

a signal to RESUME THE HOSTILITIES.

SSSSS

If PeeWee comes by and says, "What's up?"—he is a NEUTRAL OBSERVER.

If he offers to NEGOTIATE A SETTLEMENT, this is DIPLOMACY.

If he runs over to Susie to talk and runs back to tell you what she said, it's called SHUTTLE DIPLOMACY.

What PeeWee will do is MAKE PROPOSALS.

He will propose a neutral area between your castles, called a BUFFER ZONE, which Susie REJECTS.

He will propose each side give a little, called a COMPROMISE, which you REJECT.

He may propose that you ask the lifeguard (and agree to do what he decides).

This is called ARBITRATION,
which you both reject.

Or he will suggest combining your castles so you'll have the biggest castle on the beach—called A PROPOSAL ATTRACTIVE TO BOTH SIDES.

Now if you throw down your shovel, this is DISARMAMENT.

If Susie throws down her shovel, it is MUTUAL.

Hostilities are ABANDONED.

You have PEACE.